Christmas UNCUT

What really happened
and why it really matters...

Christmas Uncut
US Edition
© The Good Book Company 2012. Copyright in this edition 2013.

The Good Book Company
Tel: 0333 123 0880; International: +44 (0) 208 942 0880
Email: info@thegoodbook.com

Websites:
USA & Canada: www.thegoodbook.com
UK: www.thegoodbook.co.uk
Australia: www.thegoodbook.com.au
New Zealand: www.thegoodbook.co.nz

ISBN: 9781909559998

Design and illustration: André Parker
Printed in the US

Contents

Introduction

What did you most want the December you were six? I wanted to be one of the three kings in my nativity play. And I particularly wanted to be the king who got to wear the gold cloak. (It was actually an old curtain, but it looked good.)

Unfortunately, Mrs Abblett made the controversial decision to give out the roles based on acting ability. Since my approach to speaking on stage was "say it as loud as possible, as fast as possible," this meant the end of my kingly dream.

Instead, I got the not-so-glamorous role of the rear end of Donkey Number Two. (Luckily, it was a non-speaking part.)

And, as every six-year-old knows, there's only one donkey in the nativity story. Nowhere does it say that as Mary set out for Bethlehem, she took a spare along in case of breakdown. Or that Donkey Number One had a friend who was at a loose end that day and came along for the ride.

I was devastated. Not only was I not a main, kingly part—I wasn't even a bit-part. I was a no-part. Or, to be more accurate, the rear-end of a no-part.

No donkeys at all

But in fact, I needn't have been so disappointed. Yes, there wasn't a Donkey Number Two at the first Christmas. But here's the thing I discovered years later: *there wasn't even a Donkey Number One.* The original, real-life Mary didn't ride a donkey. And there weren't any kings, either.

The donkey and the kings are a famous part of the nativity story. But they're nowhere to be seen in the real Christmas history.

When children act out the nativity, it doesn't have much in common with the historical Christmas. Over time, we've cut huge, crucial bits out. We've added nice but completely made-up details. We've made it into a tale for children, and forgotten the real events. (Did you know that there were no kings or donkey?!)

We've turned Christmas history into a nativity play.

I don't want to be a spoilsport. Nativity plays are part of the whole Christmas experience, along with desperate last-minute shopping and sending cards to people who you didn't make the effort to see last year, and won't make the effort to see next year. If my son is ever chosen to be a king (or the back-end of a donkey, like his father before him) I will be on the front row, smiling proudly.

It's just that the real Christmas is much more interesting than what we've turned it into. It's worth rescuing and re-telling.

So let's begin. At the first Christmas, Mary wasn't waving to her mom in the front row. The angels weren't wearing last year's tinsel stuck onto old white sheets. Joseph's dad wasn't annoying a shepherd's grandma by standing up in front of her to record his son's big moment.

What there was at the first Christmas was scandal. Controversy. Massacres. Mystery.

More than history

The real Christmas is a great story. But it's more than that. This isn't simply a 2,000-year-old history; it's a story that speaks to us today—about our life, our world, our future. What happened way back then is still changing and shaping millions of people's lives in the 21st century. What really happened at Christmas still really matters today, to all of us.

That's the Christmas story this book is about. Each chapter, or scene, is in two parts. First, What really happened to real people. In each of these sections, you'll see some words in **this kind of text**. These are words taken straight out of the Bible*, and are the really important ones. Those in normal text are written by me, just to help you grasp what was going on.

And second, in Why it really matters we'll see why what happened way back then still has significance for how we live today. In each scene, this part will focus on one character from the Christmas history.

This is not a cute nativity play (though we'll mention them as we go). It's not fluffy, childish, or dull. There are some parts you probably wouldn't want a young child even to know about.

It's the real Christmas—uncut.

---

* I use sentences from the Bible to show what really happened in human history. If you want to know why, you might like to flick to "Yes, but… isn't this all made up?" at the end of the book on page 55. And if you'd like to read about the historical Christmas in the Bible, you can find it in Matthew chapter 1, verse 18 – chapter 2, verse 18; and in Luke chapter 1, verse 26 – chapter 2, verse 40.

SCENE ONE: MARY

"You will be with child... the Son of God"

It's the height of ambition for most five-year-old girls—and often their mothers, too. But in every nativity play, only one girl each year can reach the dizzying height of being asked to play Mary.

Last year, my best friend's daughter was selected. She only had one line, which she forgot, and one job, holding the baby Jesus, which she did—around the neck.

But those were minor details. She was Mary. She was proud. Her parents were proud. Everyone was happy.

Yet in a way it's strange that parents want their daughters to be Mary. We're essentially dreaming that our child will play a teenage mom who got herself pregnant in a very suspicious way, and whose life nearly fell apart because of it. Because that's what happened to the real Mary.

What really happened

To begin with, it was just a normal day: by the end, her life would have changed for ever.

But this story doesn't start with a teenage girl in northern Israel. It starts with God. It starts in heaven.

God sent the angel Gabriel to Nazareth, a town in Galilee, to a virgin pledged to be married to a man named Joseph.*

The virgin's name was Mary.

The angel went to her and said, "Greetings, you who are highly favored! The Lord is with you."

Unsurprisingly, **Mary was greatly troubled at his words and wondered what kind of greeting this might be.** She knew from the history of her people, the Jews, how rare it was for one of God's messengers to visit them; and that when an angel did appear, it usually meant things were about to get shaken up. And here she was in the middle of it all.

But the angel said to her, "Do not be afraid, Mary, you have found favor with God. You will be with child and give birth to a son.

"And you are to give him the name Jesus.

"He will be great and will be called the Son of the Most High. The Lord God will give him the throne of his father David"—the David who had ruled over Israel a thousand years earlier, and was still known and loved as the Jews' greatest ever king.

"His kingdom will never end."

Mary was in shock: but she was still able to think clearly. She was about to be pregnant—and yet she knew that was impossible.

"How will this be," Mary asked the angel, "since I am a virgin?"

The angel answered, "The Holy Spirit—God himself—will come upon you, and the power of the Most High will overshadow

---

* Words straight from the Bible are **in this kind of text**.

you. So the holy one to be born will be called the Son of God. For nothing is impossible with God."

Mary didn't fully grasp what was happening; but she knew that, for some reason, she'd just been brought into one of God's plans.

"I am the Lord's servant," Mary answered. "May it be to me as you have said."

Then the angel left her.

Explaining to Joseph what had happened wasn't easy. They hadn't slept together (they were saving it for marriage); now she was pregnant.

Joseph wasn't convinced by Mary's "God is the father" explanation; but **he was a righteous,** kind **man, and did not want to expose her to public disgrace,** to everyone knowing what she'd done with some mystery man. So **he had in mind to quietly** break up with her.

But after he had considered this, an angel of the Lord appeared to him in a dream and said, "Joseph, don't be afraid to take Mary home as your wife, because what is conceived in her is from the Holy Spirit.

"She will give birth to a son, and you are to give him the name Jesus."

Joseph knew the promises God had made to his people through the centuries. He knew God had promised that a child would be born who would in some amazing way be God himself. He knew God had said this child would be born to a virgin. And that virgin had turned out to be his girlfriend! Mary didn't deserve him leaving her; and she desperately needed him to love her.

When Joseph woke up, he did what the angel commanded him and took Mary home as his wife. But he didn't sleep with her **until she gave birth.**

> **READ THE FULL STORY** Luke 1 v 26-38; Matthew 1 v 18-25

A nativity play begins with smiles and carols. The real Christmas began with scandal, shame and shock.

Scandal

Here's the scandal. Mary was a normal girl living in a nothing town called Nazareth, in the north of Israel. She was probably 14 or 15—and (as was normal in that society) engaged to be married. But, before Joseph had touched her, she fell pregnant.

Today, that might prompt a bit of gossip, nothing more. Then, it was hugely scandalous. They took marriage seriously in Israel—so seriously that adultery could get you stoned to death.

And that's what Mary faced. Not just dirty looks and cutting comments from other women, but a lifetime of struggle and loneliness, and the real possibility of death. But they don't mention those things in nativity plays.

Shame

Here's the shame. Imagine being Joseph. Everyone would know that Mary so hated the thought of being with you that she'd decided to go elsewhere. There aren't many things more humiliating than your girl sleeping around; and that's what the neighbors would assume Mary had done. It's amazing that Joseph was prepared to split up quietly, rather than letting everyone know what Mary did. It's even more amazing that he ended up standing by her.

They don't mention those things in nativity plays, either.

Shock

And here's the shock. *All this was God's doing.*

I don't know how you imagine God, if you do at all. Maybe some old guy sitting up in the sky? Maybe some amazingly powerful force who quite frankly has more interesting things to do than care about our little lives? Maybe some distant being who really has no idea what life is actually like here on planet earth?

But here's the God of the Bible. He's a God who gets involved. Who turns lives upside down. Who doesn't act as we might expect.

He's a God who came and lived on earth, as a human.

That's the big shock. Not that a teenage girl got pregnant, and the father wasn't her boyfriend. Not that a young guy decided to stick by his girl, even though he wasn't the father.

No—the shock is that the baby "will be called the Son of God."

Who is God?

This baby was God coming to live in human history. This baby would be human (Mary was his mother); but he would also be God. He was God's Son, who had existed with God the Father (who we normally just call God) and God the Holy Spirit since before the creation of the world, since eternity.

And so here's a glimpse of who God is. He's Father, Son and Spirit. He's existed as this three-in-one God, in perfect love and relationship within himself, for eternity.

That sounds quite strange. And it is! But it's also exciting. Because if this God is all about love and relationships, then the universe he's made will be about love and relationships too. It's not about power, or possessions, or just pointlessness. The God of love and relationship has made us to enjoy a life of love which lasts and relationships that work.

That's a God worth knowing. And that's the God who was going to be born to Mary; God the Son come to live on earth.

Mindblowing

I don't know about you, but I struggle to get my head around that. The God of eternity, who knows and controls everything, becoming a baby who needs changing, feeding, burping. My mind can't work that out!

But then, there are lots of things that overload my brain—like the fact that light can travel from here to the sun in 8.3 minutes. That's a speed, according to google, of 186,000 miles per second. My mind can't really understand how something can travel so fast (science was never my strongest subject at school). But despite that, I know it does travel at that speed.

We'll never understand how God could travel so far—from his throne in heaven to the womb of a woman in Israel. But he did. The angel said that this baby "will be called the Son of God." God came to earth, as one of us, to live in the world he created.

So what will God as a human be like? What does he want to tell us? What has he come to do?

At this point, Mary had only a vague idea. But the night he was born, things would start to become clearer.

SCENE TWO: THE ANGEL

"Christ the Lord"

From the moment the couple in charge of that year's nativity decided that the children involved would make up their words, there was always a serious chance things would go wrong.

But everything began smoothly. The children were loving it—their parents (and grandparents, and aunts, and neighbors) were too. Until the angels appeared to the shepherds.

The tea-towel-head-dress-wearing five-year-old shepherds had been told that angels were not cuddly or cute—that they were, in fact, scary. And one of the shepherds had thought hard about how he would react if he saw a terrifying angel. As the blonde-haired girl playing "Chief angel," complete with white sheet and gold tinsel, appeared on stage and opened her mouth to begin speaking, he jumped up.

"#!@&*!&*#!" he shouted. "Run!" And with that, the shepherds disappeared off the stage, leaving several toy lambs and a deserted Chief angel. She announced the birth of Jesus to an empty stage.

What really happened

Mary's pregnancy went without a hitch; her labor, however, didn't.

When the Roman Emperor **Augustus issued a decree that a census should be taken of the entire Roman world,** he didn't know, and wouldn't have cared, that Mary was nine months pregnant. All his subjects had to go to their **own town to register;** and so Mary and Joseph faced an 80-mile trip **from the town of Nazareth in Galilee to Judea, to Bethlehem, the town of David, because** Joseph **belonged to the house and line of David,** who'd been king a thousand years before.

While they were there, the time came for the baby to be born, and she gave birth to her firstborn, a son. Joseph **gave him the name Jesus. She wrapped him in cloths and placed him in** an animal food trough, **because there was no room for them in the inn.**

It wasn't exactly the easiest time and place to give birth. But Mary wasn't the only person awake that night. **There were shepherds living out in the fields near by, keeping watch over their flocks at night.** They too were far from home; they too had no bed.

Being a shepherd was a dirty, boring, lonely job. Someone had to do it: and everyone else was glad it wasn't them. But it was to these shepherds that God the Father chose to announce the arrival of his Son.

An angel of the Lord appeared to them, and the glory of the Lord shone around them.

They were terrified. They knew that for centuries, coming face to face with God's glory, God's unmasked perfection, had almost always proved too much for mere people, who had died.

But the angel said to them, "Do not be afraid. I bring you good news of great joy that will be for all the people.

"Today in the town of David a Savior has been born to you; he is Christ the Lord.

"This will be a sign to you that what I'm saying is true: **You will find a baby wrapped in cloths and lying in a manger.**"

The shepherds began to pick themselves off the floor. They had seen God's glory and lived. The heavenly messengers appeared to have brought good news about a baby, not bad news about their inability to live in God's presence.

Suddenly a great company of the heavenly host of angels **appeared, praising God**.

And then, as quickly as they'd appeared, the shepherds realized **the angels had left them and gone into heaven.** Darkness returned; and all that was left was a flock of startled sheep and a few stunned shepherds.

> **READ THE FULL STORY** Luke 2 v 1-14

Why it really matters

I'd like you to meet...

How do you introduce people?

You're at a family gathering with a new boyfriend or girlfriend; or you're at a meeting with a new colleague. How do you introduce them to everyone else?

It seems to me that we usually do it by saying who they're related to, or what it is they do. It's either: "John, this is Lizzie, my girlfriend" or "Lizzie, this is John, my Grandma's nephew." Or it's: "Hannah, this is Tom, who's joined us in the marketing team" or "Tom, this is Hannah, our boss."

Family relationships and job descriptions tell you a lot about someone. And, through an angel on a hillside, God introduced his

Son to the world in exactly the same way: by outlining who he was related to, and what his job was.

Double royalty

So, who was this hours-old baby related to? "Today in the town of David," the angel said, a baby had been born, who was "the Lord."

The angel was pointing to the baby's two family trees. On one side, he was related to David, to Israel's greatest ever ruler (think of the best aspects of George Washington, Abraham Lincoln and Franklin D Roosevelt, all rolled into one). That's why Mary had to give birth on the floor of an animal shelter instead of the bed in her house. Both she and Joseph were part of David's family, which came from Bethlehem; so they'd had to travel there for the census.

David's family had fallen a long way. Joseph didn't sit on a throne in the capital, Jerusalem; he made wooden chairs in Nazareth, a rural backwater town. But God had promised that one day David's line would get their throne back. And Jesus was descended from David.

The other family tree was the one Gabriel had already told Mary about. "The Lord" is a title reserved for God; a heavenly angel, and even a lowly Jewish shepherd, would never dream of calling anyone other than God "the Lord."

God introduces Jesus as human royalty, and heavenly royalty.

Christ: not just a surname

So what job had this royal baby come to do?

"Today in the town of David a Saviour has been born to you; he is Christ the Lord."

God had given his Son Jesus two jobs. He was (still is, in fact) *Christ*.

For years, I thought "Christ" was Jesus' surname. I assumed that Joseph and Mary were Mr and Mrs Christ, and so Jesus' full name was Jesus Christ.

But actually, "Christ" is a title, not a name.

Those shepherds probably hadn't spent much time in the town's school or the local Jewish synagogue. But they would have known just how significant the arrival of God's Christ was. Christ was a title which meant God's promised King.

For centuries, God had been promising to send his King into the world. Not just any king, but *the* King. A King who would rule perfectly. A King who would rule selflessly. A King who would rule for ever.

A King whose rule would guarantee security for life, and bring satisfaction to life.

A King who would rule not only Israel, as David had, but the whole world. A King who would restore the world to how God intended, to be the perfect place he'd created.

Some King!

Over the centuries, God had given clues so that people could recognize the Christ when he finally appeared. He'd spoken through his messengers, prophets, and told his people that the Christ would be one of David's descendants. He'd told them that the Christ would be born in Bethlehem.

And now, on a hillside outside Bethlehem, he announced that, at last, the Christ had been born.

The end of disappointment

We're used to rulers disappointing us.

Think of Barack Obama storming to the Presidency in 2008. To millions, he was the one who was going to change everything. He was going to turn it all around. He was going to deliver. He was going to give the American people the life they wanted, the life they dreamed of.

Hope soon became tinged with disappointment; of course it did! How could one man change so much, do so much, achieve so much? By the time Obama was re-elected four years later, the soaring ambitions had been diluted by realism. The realization had dawned that he might make some changes... he might manage some improvements... but he couldn't deliver the hopes and dreams of millions.

He'd been asked to do too much.

Or travel to the UK and rewind back to 1997. Tony Blair had been elected Prime Minister. He was going to change things, turn it around, deliver, give the British people the life they wanted.

Unpopularity eventually arrived; of course it did! How could one imperfect man carry so many hopes? He couldn't.

He'd been asked to do too much.

And yet still we sense that we need good leadership. If only we could find someone good enough at ruling our country to give us, and everyone else, the security and satisfaction we want. Someone who was always able to know what the right thing to do was, and then was always unselfish enough to do it.

Some of us are still looking for a leader like that. Some of us have given up, deciding none of them will be good enough. Actually we're both right! Leadership *can* sort it out; but no leader we can find is the leader who *will* sort it out.

The people who lived in first-century Israel were much the same. They'd put their hopes in judges, kings, warriors, homegrown rulers and foreign emperors; none of them had delivered. They'd learned to be as cynical about leaders' promises as most of us are.

They still wanted a ruler; it was just that they had learned through experience that only a perfect man could be a perfect ruler. And they hadn't found one.

Until now. Until God's angel said to some very ordinary people: "He's here." The Christ, God's promised King, who could actually deliver on his promises, had arrived.

That was great news for those shepherds then, and it's great news for us today. There is a ruler who offers to rule us, perfectly, selflessly, for ever, giving us security throughout life and satisfaction in life. There's a ruler who can get rid of the things which stop our lives being as we'd like them to be: who can get rid of suffering, frustration, fear, even death.

There is a King who can establish endless perfection on earth. He's God's Christ, and he's the leader we're all looking for.

A strange addition

But that's not all. The angel didn't only say the Christ had been born—he added that a "Savior" had been born. The baby's job wasn't only to be a ruler, but also to be a rescuer.

Why did the people need rescuing? The answer to that question would be as shocking as the way Jesus was born; but the shepherds, and everyone else, would have to wait to find it out. For now, they started to come to terms with what had just happened out on their hillside...

SCENE THREE: THE SHEPHERDS

"Let's go and see"

The nativity play was going well. Jesus had been born, the angels had announced his birth without too much waving (and no one had run away), and now Mary and Joseph were waiting for a visit from the shepherds.

It never happened.

From the side of the stage came raised voices. Instead of walking on, the shepherds had started to argue. "I'm meant to go on first!" "No, Mrs Cole said it was my turn." Before anyone could intervene, the shepherds were using their crooks to smack each other on the head.

Soon the three young boys were in a full-on fight. Finally, a grown-up reached the battle, disentangled them, and pushed them through a door out of the hall.

The nativity play carried on. But that year, no shepherds visited the baby.

What really happened

The shepherds said to one another, "Let's go to Bethlehem and see this thing that has happened, which the Lord has told us about."

So they hurried off and found Mary and Joseph, and the baby, who was lying in the manger. It was just as they had been told.

When they had seen him, they spread the word concerning what had been told them about this child. Of course, everyone who heard it was amazed at what the shepherds said to them.

The shepherds themselves **returned** to their sheep and their fields and the darkness. Those things were just the same as they'd been several hours before; but life wasn't.

God could have chosen a royal palace to announce Jesus' birth, or a religious temple. He hadn't; he'd picked their field! They spent the rest of the night **glorifying and praising God for all the things they had heard and seen.**

Mary was simply exhausted. She knew the events of the past 24 hours were of life-changing, world-shaping significance. She also knew it would take a long time, perhaps her whole life, to process what had gone on. She **treasured up all these things and pondered them in her heart.**

> **READ THE FULL STORY** Luke 2 v 15-20

Why it really matters

If God's Christ, God's Son, has really come to live in this world, that's of huge significance. It means we can know what God is like. It means we can know what God thinks of us. It means we can know how God designed us to live, the way which makes us happiest.

If God's Christ was born and laid in a manger in Bethlehem, it's huge—for all people, in every place and in every time.

So the vital question for the shepherds was: Is it true? Had the angel made it up? Had they made the angel up?! Was it all a dream, a mistake, a joke?

There was only one way to find out for sure. Sensibly, they said to each other: "Let's go to Bethlehem and see." The angel had told them they'd find a baby, wrapped in cloths and lying, slightly strangely, in a manger, a food trough for animals.

They could go and look for themselves. Either this baby in a manger would be there, or he wouldn't. Either Jesus the Christ had been born, or he hadn't. It was a question of fact.

Fact—or false

This is one of the great things about Christianity. You might think it's all true; or you might be very doubtful. But Christianity is about historical fact. In the end, it's not about feelings, or what you were brought you up to believe, or finding some secret knowledge; it's about facts of history.

Either the Christ was born, that night, in that town, and put in that manger as angels announced his birth to some shepherds—in which case, he's God's promised perfect King. Or, Jesus wasn't born as they said—in which case Christianity's false, made up, and not worth your time.

Check—don't assume

When the shepherds looked into it, they discovered it was all "just as they had been told." What they found in Bethlehem backed up the angel's claims on the hillside. It had happened. They checked it out, and found it was fact.

In the 21st century, many people just assume that Christianity is false. They don't check; they assume. Equally, some people just assume that the whole Jesus Christ thing is true, without thinking about it; and often, when their views are challenged, their faith falls over.

When I trained as a journalist, the man who taught us had been a sub-editor for years. He was a small guy who had grown up in Wales and had a strong Welsh accent. He had two favorite lines, which I can still hear him saying as I write this.

One was: "That's useless (actually, he used a stronger, shorter word). Bin it!"

The other was: "Assume makes a donkey (again, he used a stronger, shorter word) out of u and me."

Time and again, he told us that opinions don't matter much. What people *think* is irrelevant. What counts is *facts*. Don't assume you know the truth, he insisted. Check out the facts: what really happened?

That's what the shepherds did. And they found it was true.

Unfortunately, we're 2,000 years too late to go and see the manger for ourselves. But we can still make sure we don't just assume one way or the other. Is it facts, or false? We can see whether Luke, the writer who tells us about the shepherds, was writing historical facts. We can see whether his story matches what else we know about that part of history. We can read the rest of his biography of Jesus and see if it has the ring of truth to it.

We can look into whether what happened at the beginning of Jesus' life is fact. And we can explore whether what happened at the end—when he died and then rose again—is really fact too.

I know people who, when they've begun to look into the Gospels' claims about Jesus, have been surprised by what they've found. I know that I was, when I began to look into it.

If you want to follow the shepherds and check out if it's true, the best place to start is by grabbing a copy of Luke's biography, or "Gospel," about Jesus. And if you want to know more about why we can confidently treat Luke's Gospel as history, page 55 will get you started and point you to some other stuff to read which goes into more detail.

But for now, we need to leave the shepherds in their fields. Because the story's focus switches to a mysterious country hundreds of miles from the manger and the baby.

SCENE FOUR: THE MAGI

"We have come to worship him"

The first wise man, a seven-year-old boy, was really psyched to be wearing a crown on stage, with everyone looking at him. He said his line, and knelt down next to the manger to offer his gift to Jesus.

Then there was a pause.

He looked at the box in his hands, wrapped in beautiful, shiny gold paper. He began to look doubtful, and to shuffle away from the manger.

"Give the baby Jesus your present," hissed the organizer from the edge of the stage, where she was trying to convince an angel not to pull her wings off her costume.

The wise man shook his head.

"Give Jesus your gift," said the organizer, striding on to the stage and attempting to pry the boy's fingers off the present.

"No," squealed the wise man. "It's my gold box, and I'm keeping it."

Although the Romans were in overall charge, they let a local guy rule Israel as king, to keep the peace and keep the taxes coming in.

When Jesus was born, it was **the time of King Herod.** And some time after the night Jesus was born, **Magi,** or wise men, **from the east came to Jerusalem and asked, "Where is the one who has been born king of the Jews? We saw his star in the east and have come to worship him."**

These men were a wise, intelligent, sensible group. If the king of the Jews had come along, it made sense to look in the Jewish capital. But he wasn't there—and the star they'd followed from their own country seemed to have disappeared from the sky. They kept asking around—and eventually news of these strange foreigners looking for a new-born king reached the royal palace.

When King Herod heard this he was disturbed, and all Jerusalem with him. When he had called together all the chief priests and teachers of the law, he asked them where the Christ was to be born.

This was an easy question for the religious leaders. They knew their Scriptures back to front. They knew what God had promised about the coming Christ through his human messengers, or prophets. And they knew what God had told one of those prophets, Micah, seven hundred years earlier.

"In Bethlehem in Judea," they replied, "for this is what the prophet has written:

> **'But you, Bethlehem, in the land of Judah, are by no means least among the rulers of Judah; for out of you will come a ruler who will be the shepherd of my people Israel.'"**

Then Herod called the Magi secretly and found out from them the exact time the star had appeared. He was guessing these easterners had spotted the star when the baby was born: and he wanted to know how old this Christ was by now.

He sent them to Bethlehem and said, "Go and make a careful search for the child. As soon as you find him, report to me, so that I too may go and worship him."

After they had heard the king, they went on their way, and the star they had seen in the east went ahead of them until it stopped over the place where the child was. When they saw the star, they were overjoyed.

On coming to the house, they saw the child with his mother Mary, and they bowed down and worshiped him.

Then they opened their treasures and presented him with gifts of gold and of incense and of myrrh. They had found the one they'd traveled so far to see.

> **READ THE FULL STORY** Matthew 2 v 1-11

Why it really matters

Baby visitors

Do you know who visited you after you were born? According to my mom (I've heard this story several times now), I was visited by my dad, my grandparents, a couple of nurses, a doctor and Linda, a lady who was in hospital having a baby too.

In other words, my birth was so significant that I was visited by people who were members of my family, or people who were in the hospital anyway.

But, as far as I'm aware, President Ronald Reagan was not even informed that Carl Laferton had just entered the world. The professors of Harvard, Yale, Oxford and Cambridge Universities did not pack their bags and come racing to the hospital to peer over the side of my cradle. Once I got home, at no stage did Queen Elizabeth II of Great Britain knock on the door and ask my parents if she could give me some presents.

Of course they didn't. It would have been ridiculous, foolish, for them to do so. The powerful and the intelligent people of 1981 AD would have been crazy to have dropped everything, cleared their schedules, and come to see me so that they could get on their knees and worship me.

Wise? No: stupid!

But that's exactly what these "wise men" did in around 0 AD. We don't know much about them: we don't know where they came from except "the east"; we don't know what they were called; we don't actually know how many of them there were. We don't even quite know what they did—the word "Magi" suggests they were either some kind of professor or some kind of local ruler, or a bit of both.

But what we do know is that these men traveled hundreds of miles, for months and months, with expensive gifts, to see… a baby born in a small town in an insignificant country in a far corner of an empire.

What we do know is that when they got to the house where Mary was staying with Jesus (it seems he'd been upgraded from a manger to a proper cradle), these powerful, intelligent men got down on their knees and worshiped this child. "We have come to worship him," they had told King Herod—and that's exactly what they did.

That's ridiculous. Stupid. Crazy.

Well, it would have been, if it hadn't been for the fact that, as we've seen, this child was different. This child had been born "king of the Jews," the Christ himself. And, though these wise men weren't Jews, they knew this child mattered for them too.

If Jesus is the Christ, then what these Magi did wasn't ridiculous or stupid or crazy. It was really very sensible. If Jesus is the Christ, the right response is to worship him.

And that goes for us, too.

We, like the wise men, probably aren't from Israel. We may not know very much about what God's prophets said (though we can find their words in the Old Testament). We may tend to look to the stars and guess at what's going on, instead of simply reading what God says in his Bible.

But if Jesus is the Christ, the right response is to copy the Magi—and worship him.

What is worship?

But what does "worship" mean? For years, I thought it meant going to church, being fairly dull, and possibly wearing sandals. But the Magi show us it's something quite different.

It means giving up our time for Jesus, just as they did.

It means putting ourselves out for Jesus; asking for more knowledge about Jesus; giving Jesus the best we have to offer—just as they did.

It means letting Jesus shape how we use our days, our minds, our wallets.

In other words, it means letting Jesus be the center of our lives.

And, crucially, it means accepting that Jesus is our Christ, our ruler—just as they did.

The wise option

Lots of people think you have to be a bit stupid to worship Jesus.

But these "wise men" would probably say it's wiser to accept that God became a man called Jesus, than to ignore him. And that it's wiser to accept that if we can't understand everything about Jesus, maybe it's not because we're clever and it's all rubbish, but because he's God and we're not.

Perhaps the wise thing to do is to look at the evidence and think things through, instead of dismissing anything to do with God's promised perfect King.

And if Jesus is the Christ, perhaps the wise thing to do is to worship him with all we have, just as those rulers did.

It's what wise rulers have been doing ever since. Queen Victoria, who as British monarch in the nineteenth century ruled over a third of the world, said she could not wait to meet Jesus. Why? "So that I can cast my crown before him." She recognized that even as one of the most powerful people in the world, she had a ruler, one who deserved her everything—even her crown.

But not all rulers react to Jesus being the Christ in quite the same way. And, as the Magi bowed down to Jesus in Bethlehem, back in Jerusalem one king was planning to do something very different to him…

SCENE FIVE: KING HEROD

"Kill all the boys"

The year after I played a donkey's rear-end, I hit the big time. I was chosen to be King Herod. I had to shout and scowl and stamp my feet—a role that used the full range of my acting abilities.

But my lines missed out a huge chunk of what happened in history. There's a part that never appears in children's nativity plays. Even lots of churches skip over it with their adults each December. After all, massacres don't play too well with parents, and aren't too popular at festive services.

This is where Christmas history gets darker…

What really happened

When the Magi had met and bowed down to Jesus, **they returned to their country by a different route,** because they had **been warned in a dream not to go back to Herod.**

They weren't the only people leaving Bethlehem. **When they had gone, an angel of the Lord appeared to Joseph in a dream.**

"Get up," he said, "take the child and his mother and escape to Egypt. Stay there until I tell you, for Herod is going to search for the child to kill him."

Joseph did as he was told. He got up, took the child and his mother during the night and left for Egypt.

When Herod realized that he had been outwitted by the Magi, he was furious, and he gave orders to kill all the boys in Bethlehem and its vicinity who were two years old and under, in accordance with the time he had learned from the Magi.

Herod's orders were carried out to the letter. Bethlehem was marked by weeping and great mourning, with the women refusing to be comforted. It was a massacre.

But Herod failed to achieve his aim. God's Son Jesus was in Egypt, where he stayed until the death of Herod. After Herod died, an angel of the Lord appeared in a dream to Joseph in Egypt and said, "Get up, take the child and his mother and go to the land of Israel, for those who were trying to take the child's life are dead."

So he got up, and went to the land of Israel. He went and lived in Nazareth. Finally, Joseph, Mary and Jesus were home.

> **READ THE FULL STORY** Matthew 2 v 12-23

Why it really matters

Mass grave

It's a horrific, shocking twist—the cold-blooded murder of what would have been dozens of toddlers.

There must have been a mass grave near Bethlehem, one filled with the small bodies of children. We see such graves from time to time on television; I once even visited a mass grave in which some of my relatives are buried. It's a tragic fact that a massacre like this is not an infrequent event through human history.

And the question is: why? Why did Herod dislike Jesus so much that he wanted to kill him? Why was Herod prepared to kill any number of boys just to be sure he'd taken out one particular toddler?

Turf war

The answer to that question is one we might not like, because it involves us. The answer is that what we're watching in this episode of the Christmas story is a turf war.

Herod was king of Israel; it was his country. He ruled it. Yes, he ruled it under the Romans, but most of the time he could ignore that fact. Israel was his.

But now the Christ had been born. God's King of the Jews had arrived. And ultimately, Israel belonged to him (the whole world did). Jesus had the greatest claim to be the ruler of Israel. Not the Romans. Not Herod.

So Herod had a decision to make.

He could, like Queen Victoria did 1800 years later, accept that Jesus was the king over him. He could carry on being king, but under Jesus' authority, taking the decisions Jesus wanted him to, allowing his life to be shaped by Jesus. He could give his turf, his Israel, to Jesus, worshiping him as Christ.

Or Herod could resist Jesus. He could fight Jesus. He could push Jesus out of Israel, so that he could carry on being the only ruler.

He chose the second option. He tried to get rid of Jesus; that's why Bethlehem's toddlers were massacred. The action of mass murder was motivated by Herod's attitude of refusing to let Jesus be his ruler.

That attitude is what the Bible calls "sin." It's the attitude which resists Jesus' rule, which would rather Jesus didn't exist, which refuses to accept that Jesus, God's Christ, is the rightful ruler.

It's the attitude which says: "This is my turf, Jesus, not yours. I will not let you have it. I will fight you."

Herod and me

Herod had a lot of turf—the whole of Israel. I don't have much at all—but I do have my own life. In my life, in what I do and say and how I treat people, I'm the ruler. It's mine.

Except that if Jesus is the Christ—if he's God's Son who created me and created the world I live in—then actually my life belongs to him. He has the greatest claim to say how I should live and what I should do and how I should treat others in his world. He has a greater claim than anyone else, a greater claim even than mine.

So when it comes to the turf of my own life, I have a choice. I can accept Jesus' rule, worshiping him as my king—like the Magi. Or I can resist and refuse his rule—like Herod.

Naturally, I choose the second option.

I rule my own life. I sin. Because I was brought up to have manners, I do it quite politely: I'm not rude about Jesus, I'm often quite nice to other people, I work hard. Sometimes, when what Jesus says happens to agree with what I already think, I do what he'd like. But at the end of the day, I want me to be in charge of life, not Jesus.

So I act as if he isn't the King. I act as if he's dead.

Herod and us

And the hard truth is that this is what we all do, naturally. When it comes to the turf of our own lives, we are all mini-Herods.

That doesn't lead us to ruin people's lives through committing mass murder. But our refusal to let Jesus be our ruler does lead us to ruin others' lives in smaller, less noticeable ways. The person whose heart we selfishly broke, who can't quite put it behind them. The person we laughed at, shattering their confidence. The person we trod on to get a promotion at work, who's now twisted by bitterness. The person we simply never noticed and unconsciously ignored, who feels lonely and worthless. The little things we do each day which make the lives of those around us a bit less satisfying than God wants them to be.

I wish this didn't describe me. I wish I could look at my life and truthfully say I've never acted in those ways. But when I'm honest, I know that I can't. I'm guessing you can't, either.

And all these outward actions (and many others) are signs of an inward attitude—an attitude that looks at our life and looks at Jesus Christ and says: "This is my turf, Jesus, not yours. I will not let you have it."

It's a hard truth to accept; but it explains what we see in the world around us, and it explains what we sometimes notice in our own hearts. We're sinful, just like Herod.

And, just like Herod, we're fighting a turf war that we can't win.

A losing battle

Herod must have thought he had all the power: he had priests to advise him, wise men to inform him, soldiers to kill for him. But he couldn't do what he wanted; he couldn't kill Jesus off. Because compared to God, he had no power at all. God was in control—sending angels, speaking through dreams, moving his Son to safety.

King Herod tried hard to get rid of God's King; but he couldn't. And by the time Joseph brought his family back to Nazareth, only one of those two kings was still alive—and it wasn't Herod. The turf Herod had killed to keep was taken away from him.

I wonder what God said to Herod when he died? I wonder if Herod tried to find a way to excuse how he'd treated God's Son, and how he'd treated others as he fought God's Son? I doubt there was anything he could say.

And, like Herod, we can resist Jesus' right to rule throughout our whole lives if we choose to. But, however powerful we are, we can't resist him for ever. Just as it did for Herod, the time will come when each of us dies.

I wonder what you're planning to say to God beyond your death? Is there any possible excuse you and I will be able to offer for how we've treated God's Son, and how we've treated others as we've fought him?

It won't help to argue that our actions have been less serious than others'. Or that we did some good things among the bad. Or that we had thought about Jesus from time to time—or even that we believed he was quite special.

Our sinfulness means that none of us will deserve a place in the kingdom of the Christ we've rejected. There will be no eternity enjoying all his goodness and gifts—of which the best of this life is just a tiny glimpse. Instead, there will be an eternity outside his kingdom, enduring an existence with nothing good in it at all—of which the worst of this life is just a glimmer.

This is a hard truth—it makes death something to be terrified of. It's an unpopular truth—but that doesn't stop it being true. I need rescuing from the consequences of my rejection of Jesus, the Christ. We all do. So it's great to remember what the angel said to those shepherds: "Today in the town of David a Savior has been born".

Jesus was born not only to rule us, but to rescue us. And it would be the end of his life, not the beginning, which would show what the angel had meant.

SCENE SIX: SIMEON

"A sword will pierce your own soul"

There's only one old man who gets a mention at Christmas. He wears red... brings the presents... and, bizarrely, often pops up at random points in nativity plays. Santa Claus may not be real (sorry if that's news to you) but he's pretty popular.

Of course, Santa was nowhere to be seen at the first Christmas. But there was an old man at the heart of the real events. Not Santa, but Simeon. And Simeon didn't do presents.

But he did do predictions...

What really happened

As tradition demanded, Mary and Joseph brought Jesus to the temple in Jerusalem **to present him to the Lord and to offer a sacrifice** in recognition that their baby was, as all babies are, a gift from God to them.

There was a man in Jerusalem called Simeon. It had been revealed to him by the Holy Spirit that he would not die before he had seen the Lord's Christ.

That day, he went into the temple courts. When the parents brought in the child Jesus, Simeon took him in his arms and praised God, saying:

"Sovereign Lord, as you have promised, you now dismiss your servant in peace. For my eyes have seen your salvation."

Then Simeon said to Mary, his mother: "This child is destined to be spoken against, so that the thoughts of many hearts will be revealed.

"And a sword will pierce your own soul too."

It was a strange, unsettling prediction. And three decades later, Mary discovered just what he had meant. A few hundreds yards from where Simeon had held her son in his arms, Mary watched as soldiers executed him. She'd sat next to Jesus' manger; now, thirty years later, she was standing next to his cross.

When Jesus saw his mother there, and one of his closest friends, John, standing nearby, he said to his mother, "Dear woman, here is your son," and to John, "Here is your mother."

From that time on, John took her into his home to care for her as part of his family.

From all around the cross, the mockery and insults rained down on the dying man. The religious leaders had hated Jesus ever since he started explaining that he was the Christ. So they'd spread lies to have him found guilty, and were enjoying getting rid of him:

"He saved others; let him save himself if he is the Christ of God, the Chosen One."

He didn't save himself; he stayed nailed to the wooden cross. But as Jesus hung there—mocked, naked and bleeding—something strange happened above him.

It was now about midday, **and darkness came over the land, for the sun stopped shining.** This wasn't some kind of natural eclipse—the timing was wrong for that. It was strange... and it was significant. As the Jews who were watching knew, God had already explained it. Centuries before he had warned them—the people he'd lived with, looked after and spoken to—that he wouldn't go on putting up with their sin, with their determination not to live with him as God.

He warned them that a day was coming when he'd pour out his anger at the way people had treated each other, his world, and him. Since they'd rejected living with God as their King, he'd reject them from being in his eternal kingdom. He'd take away all the good things they'd enjoyed from him without ever thinking of or thanking him.

God had promised that: **"In that day, I will make the sun go down at noon and darken the earth in broad daylight."**

Now God's right anger, his punishment, had come.

And yet, apart from the darkness, everything seemed normal. Perhaps it was a false alarm! People relaxed, carrying on with their daily business.

The darkness lasted for three hours.

Then, **with a loud cry, Jesus breathed his last. One of the soldiers pierced Jesus' side with a spear, bringing a sudden flow of blood and water.**

God's Christ, the man Jesus, Mary's son, was dead. And, her soul pierced, she stood there, **watching these things.**

> **READ THE FULL STORY** Luke 2 v 21-40, 23 v 44-49; John 19 v 25-37; Mark 15 v 25-41; Amos 8 v 9-14

The piercing sword

One of the worst things in the world is to be a parent whose child dies. Someone once wrote that it's like losing a leg: you get used to it, but the loss and the pain never really go.

Mary didn't only know what it was like to have her son die. She knew what it was like to *watch* her son die. She knew an unimaginable grief—what that old man Simeon had described thirty years earlier, while holding her baby, as having a sword pierce her soul.

She must have felt that emotional sword as Jesus—who'd lived a blameless life but was killed because the Jewish leaders didn't want him to be their Christ—had real six-inch nails hammered through his wrists and his ankles.

She must have felt that emotional sword as Jesus had a real spear pushed through his side.

And she must have felt that emotional sword as Jesus hung on the cross as the sky went black; as her son experienced a spiritual torment far worse than either his physical pain or his mother's emotional pain.

The anger of God

The sky going black as the Jewish leaders killed God's Christ should be of no surprise. The darkness signaled that God's anger had come. Of course God the Father was angry! His own Son, who he loved, was being unfairly executed. Wouldn't you be angry?

The surprise is not that God the Father was angry; the surprise is *who* God was angry with. His anger and his punishment didn't fall on the men who'd fought a turf war against his Christ. They didn't die. No, God the Father's anger and punishment fell on the man who was his Christ. His anger fell on his Son—on the only man of his day, of any day, who had never done anything wrong. The shock is that *Jesus* died.

On the cross, God the Son chose to bear the punishment that people deserve for their sin, for their refusal to let Christ rule. Jesus experienced the hell of being shut out of his Father's kindness and kingdom. He traded places. He was punished instead of sinful people.

God's Son took God's anger so that we don't have to.

What the cross shows

Stand next to Mary for a moment, and watch the Christ dying under God's punishment. His agony on the cross shows us how horrific life without God is. It shows us what you and I face beyond death for trying to push him out of the turf of our lives: a future outside Christ's kingdom.

But his cross also shows us that this doesn't need to be our future. When we die, instead of standing before God with nothing to say and no excuses to make, we can stand there and say:

> "The Christ I resisted took hell instead of me. The Christ I resisted saved me from hell. The Christ I resisted has given me a place in his perfect kingdom."

When the angel told those shepherds that "a Savior has been born to you ... Christ the Lord," he was pointing to the cross. The baby lying in a manger at the first Christmas had come to hang on the cross on the first Good Friday. Jesus came not only to rule people, but to rescue them. Not only to tell people about his eternal perfect kingdom, but to make a way for sinful people like us to get into that kingdom.

He came to be the Savior. He chose to die so that our death does not need to be a terrifying dead-end, the end of all hope and joy and peace. It can be the doorway to perfect life in Christ's kingdom.

God's script

It's ironic, when you think about it. God the Father was in control at Jesus' birth, so Herod's attempts to kill him failed. And God the Father was still in control at Jesus' death, which is the only reason the religious leaders' attempts to kill him succeeded. The script had been written not in a palace or a temple but in heaven.

God the Most High was in control of every detail. And he was in control three days later when Mary's sister-in-law and some other women went to the tomb Jesus was buried in. They went to rub spices into his body to stop it smelling in the heat.

But they didn't find a corpse.

Instead, just as Mary had seen all those years ago at home in Nazareth as a teenager, they saw an angel.

And **the angel said to the women, "You are looking for Jesus, who was crucified. He is not here; he has risen, just as he said. Come and see the place where he lay."**

So the women hurried away from the tomb, afraid yet filled with joy, and ran to tell his disciples. Suddenly Jesus met them.

"Greetings," he said.

They came to him, clasped his feet and (just as the Magi had thirty years before) **worshiped him.***

Mary knew what it was to watch her son die. But amazingly, she also knew what it was to have a son rise from the dead. God's plan had always been for his Son to be born as the Christ, the Ruler; to die to be people's Savior, the Rescuer; and to rise to eternal life beyond death so that he can welcome people who worship him into perfect life in his kingdom.

* **READ THE FULL STORY** Matthew 28 v 1-20

SCENE SEVEN: JESUS

"Repent and believe"

It was a big event for everyone involved. A nativity performed in a big venue, with local VIPs and the press attending. It was hard work helping the children learn their lines, making costumes, and working out who would play Mary. But now all was ready, the guests gathered, and the nativity began.

It was only now that the organizers realized something was missing. One of them had left the doll playing Jesus back at home. Miles away. And there was no time.

Fortunately, in nativity plays you don't really need Jesus. He has no lines. The focus is on the other characters—Mary and Joseph, the angels, shepherds, Magi. Afterwards, the teachers weren't sure whether anyone had even noticed that there had been no Jesus in the manger that year.

What really happened

When he was around thirty, **Jesus went into Galilee,** the area around Nazareth, **proclaiming the good news of God.**

"The time has come," he said. **"The kingdom of God is near. Repent and believe the good news!"**

> **READ THE FULL STORY** Mark 1 v 1-20

Why it really matters

There are four historical biographies, or Gospels, of Jesus in the Bible. One of them was written by a very early follower of Jesus, a man named Mark. And the startling thing about his Gospel is that he completely ignores the Christmas story!

Mark misses out the angels, the shepherds, the Magi. There's no mention of Jesus' parents, his birth, or his childhood.

Perhaps Mark wants us to remember that the baby grew up. Perhaps he wants to put the man Jesus center-stage, for us to hear what he said and what he did. Perhaps he doesn't want to leave us the option of pretending Jesus stayed a baby, who never said or did anything.

Mark takes us straight to Jesus the man. And the first words he records Jesus saying sum up why Jesus was born, and why he died, and why it really matters for each one of us:

> "The time has come. The kingdom of God is near. Repent and believe the good news!"

"The time has come"

With Jesus, God breaks into history as a human. There's no need to guess who he is. The time has come for us to know. There's no need to wonder if God will ever sort out this world. The time has come for him to do it.

"The kingdom of God is near"

With Jesus, the perfect kingdom of God begins to be built. In what he did—in how he healed people, how he welcomed people, how he loved people—Jesus gave a glimpse of how amazing life in his kingdom is. In how he died—how he took the punishment of God that we deserve, experienced the hell that we should experience—Jesus gave us a way to be part of his kingdom for ever.

The perfect, fulfilling, satisfying life—the life that we're all, one way or another, striving to find—was offered to us at the first Christmas.

The time has come to know God. The perfect kingdom of God has been opened up for anyone to enjoy—including you. But how do we grab hold of it? Two things...

"Repent"

This is a Roman military word, meaning "about turn." To "repent" is to turn around completely. To be part of his kingdom, now and beyond death, Jesus says you need to repent; you need to turn away from living with yourself as ruler, and towards living with him as your King.

Repenting means giving your life to Jesus, and worshiping him: letting him call the shots, looking to him when you make decisions, leaving it to him to tell you how to act.

Repenting is a great thing to do. It means the ruler of your life will no longer be someone who doesn't actually know that much about life, and who knows nothing about the future (ie: you!). Instead, the one in charge of you will be someone who knows everything about life, and who controls the future—Jesus the Christ, the Son of God.

But repenting is a hard thing to do. It means you won't simply do what you want, or what's easiest, or what's most popular any more. You won't be in charge of your schedule, your wallet, your heart. It means there will be times when you want to disagree with what Jesus says, but obey him anyway. And there will be times when you seem to be missing out.

If you know someone who's repented—who lives as a Christian— you'll know they make some decisions that seem quite strange. They often don't do things that most people say make you feel good in life. And yet you'll probably also have noticed that they seem more satisfied and more secure than people who are chasing wealth, promotion, sex or power.

"Believe the good news"

Everybody trusts in things. If you're sitting down to read this, you're currently trusting in your chair or sofa—you believe it will bear your weight. If you're married, you're trusting in your husband or wife to mean it when they say they love you and are faithful to you. If you work for a living, you're trusting you'll get paid.

What are you trusting in for your death? What or who are you trusting will sort your death out for you? Maybe it's yourself—you believe that being a pretty nice person will mean it's all OK. Maybe it's an idea—you believe there's nothing the other side of death, so you don't need to worry.

Christians believe in "good news" about a person. Someone who knows what's on the other side of death because he's been there. Someone who knows how to get through death because he's done it.

The "good news" of the Bible is that Jesus has done everything necessary to give you perfect life in God's eternal kingdom. You don't need to try to gain it yourself. You don't need to be good enough. You don't need to go to church a certain number of times. You don't need to keep lots of religious rules.

You just need to "believe the good news"—to trust that Jesus the Christ has done it all for you. That when he died, he died in your place, taking the punishment from God you deserve. That when he rose, he rose to give you life in his kingdom.

How about *you*?

So, when Jesus calls people to repent and believe, he's calling them to accept him as their Ruler—the one who's in charge of their life—and their Rescuer—the one who will bring them through death.

In some ways, it'd be easier for us if Jesus had never said anything— if he'd stayed quiet in his manger and never grown up. But he did grow up, and he does speak. He tells us that in him we can see God and see God's kingdom. He challenges me, and you, to repent and believe.

I can still remember the evening years ago when someone asked me: What are you going to do about Jesus? By that point, I'd understood for a while what really happened; that Jesus had really existed, had lived and died and risen in history. And slowly, I'd come to see that these were not just historical details, like the date World War Two started or the Berlin Wall came down—that Jesus' life really mattered.

But I hadn't done anything about it. It had made no difference to my life or to my future. Until that friend of mine said: What are you going to do about Jesus?

It was a blunt question! But I suddenly realized that it had an obvious answer. I needed to repent and believe, to accept Jesus as my Ruler and my Rescuer. It was no good just knowing about him; I needed to actually know him, to start following and trusting in and speaking to and listening to him.

It was the most important decision I ever made. In many ways, it was a decision that made my life more difficult. But in every way, it has made my life more fulfilling, satisfying and exciting. Looking back, it was easily the best decision I've ever made.

So, I'll finish this last chapter with that same blunt question: What are *you* going to do about Jesus?

Maybe you need to think things through a bit more, to do some checking out of the facts, to ask some questions. Over the page, there are a few ways you could do that.

But maybe you know that the time has come for you to make the decision—to repent and believe. You know the time has come to tell Jesus you want him to be your Ruler and your Rescuer. In other words, to become a Christian.

Why not speak to him now?

What next?

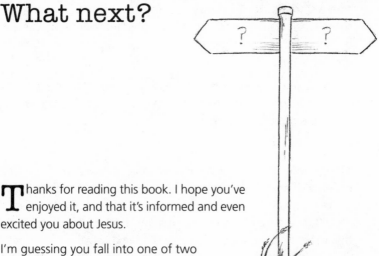

Thanks for reading this book. I hope you've enjoyed it, and that it's informed and even excited you about Jesus.

I'm guessing you fall into one of two categories:

Maybe you're *someone who would like to keep looking into Christianity* before making your mind up about what you believe. Here are a few ways you can keep thinking things through…

Read a Gospel. There are four historical biographies of Jesus' life—Matthew, Mark, Luke and John (this book has used parts of all of them). Why not grab one and read through it? The shortest one is Mark, which takes around two hours to read.

Pray. Speak to God, and ask him, if he is there, to help you to see the truth about who he is, who Jesus is, and what life is all about.

Go to a website. *www.christianityexplored.org* allows you to keep thinking about Jesus in your own way, at your own pace, in your own time. It features an animation which explains who Jesus is, why he came, and what it means for us; some video answers to questions lots of people ask; and some real-life stories of people who thought things through themselves. And on the site, you can also find out about how you can…

Join a Christianity Explored course. This is an informal, relaxed, seven-week walk through the Gospel of Mark, where you can ask questions, discuss, or simply listen. You can find a course near you on the website.

Look at the historical evidence. If you'd like to look in more detail at how we know that the Gospels are real history, a great book to read is *The Case for Christmas*, by Lee Strobel.

Maybe, though, you're reading this page as ***someone who has repented and believed***—you've become a Christian. That's fantastic! It can all seem a bit strange at first (or at least, it did for me). The best advice I can give you is to **find a church** near you that bases all it says on the Bible (in the same way this book does). The people there will help you get on with enjoying knowing Jesus, your Ruler and Rescuer, and encourage you to see how you can worship him. If you'd like a hand with finding a church like this, just email info@thegoodbook.com.

Yes, but...

isn't this all made up?

When you read something, it helps to know what you're reading. I wouldn't use a car manual to tell me how to cook a roast dinner; I wouldn't use a recipe book to help me change my car's oil!

Throughout this book, you'll have seen me talking about what the four "Gospels" in the Bible tell us about what really happened at the first Christmas. And I talk about what they say as though those things really happened; as though they were history. Why?

Because that's the type of books the Gospels are. Here's how one of them, written by a man called Luke, begins:

Many have undertaken to draw up an account of the things that have been fulfilled among us, just as they were handed down to us by those who from the first were eye-witnesses and servants of the word.

Therefore, since I myself have carefully investigated everything from the beginning, it seemed good also to me to write an orderly account for you, most excellent Theophilus, so that you may know the certainty of the things you have been taught.

Luke was writing his Gospel about Jesus for someone he knew, a guy called Theophilus. And what he wanted to do was to let Theophilus know what had actually happened to Jesus. He'd researched it all, he'd spoken to eyewitnesses who'd seen what really happened: now he'd written it all out in an "orderly" way.

He was writing a historical biography of Jesus' life. That's his claim.

Now of course, Luke could have just made it all up, just as I could rewrite history to make my dad an NFL star player instead of a retired computer science teacher. But it's completely unlikely that Luke would have done that, for two reasons.

First, at the time Luke (and the other Gospel writers) were writing their historical biographies of Jesus, you could very easily get killed for being a Christian. Why make up something that could land you in prison, facing torture and death?! It would be like me making up a back-story for my dad which claimed that he was a high-level al-Qaeda terrorist, and that I was working for him.

Second, Luke was a Christian. It's easy to think that would make it more likely that he'd make his Gospel up. Actually, it makes it less likely. If Luke thought this guy Jesus was God, he'd really, really care about getting the facts about him correct. He wouldn't want to make mistakes about someone so important. He'd be more careful to tell historical fact, not less.

One final thing that can make us even more confident that Luke and the others are telling us historical facts is that their stories fit with other historical accounts of the time. The events they talk about fit with other histories. The people they talk about, like Roman emperors and Jewish priests, are real people. Jesus himself is mentioned by both Roman and Jewish historians who would probably rather he hadn't lived; so he himself definitely existed. And the details of the places they wrote about, like how there were two towns next to each other with the same name, check out with archaeological research.

Which means that the Gospels claim to be historical fact; they sound like historical fact; and they check out with other histories as historical fact. Which is why, in this book, I treat what they say about Jesus as historical fact. Strange facts, amazing facts, challenging facts, but still facts!

If you'd like to think about in more detail about why we can be confident that the Gospels are history, a couple of short, great books to read are: *Is the Bible True... Really?* by Josh McDowell, or *The Case for Christ* by Lee Strobel.

Yes, but...

was Jesus really the Christ?

Today, we want our sons to find a cure for cancer, or play sport professionally. In those days presumably every Jew hoped their son would be the Christ, God's King.

So... how do we know Joseph and Mary didn't just claim Jesus was the Christ, and manage to convince people to believe them and treat him as God's King?

This is where what God said before Jesus was born is really helpful. For literally centuries, he'd been telling people how they could know for sure whether or not someone really was his Christ.

So he said through one prophet, or messenger, of his: **"The virgin will be with child, and will give birth to a son, and will call him 'God with us'"** (Isaiah chapter 7 verse 13, written 700 years before Jesus was born).

Through another, he said: **"Bethlehem ... out of you will come for me one who will be ruler over Israel, whose origins are from of old"** (Micah 5 v 2, 700 years before Jesus was born).

And it wasn't just the manner and place of his birth that God predicted. He told how his Christ would die, too:

"All who see me mock me: they hurl insults, shaking their heads ... they have pierced my hands and my feet ... they divide my garments among them and cast lots for my clothing" (Psalm 22 v 7, 16, 18—1,000 years before Jesus was born).

If you're reading this before you read chapter six, then I hope it's not spoiling the story, but that's exactly how Jesus died: mocked by those around him, pierced by nails on a cross, with his clothing being gambled for by soldiers.

There are loads more prophecies like these. But here's the thing: Joseph and Mary couldn't have organized the whole of Jesus' life to fulfil these things. And Jesus certainly couldn't have sorted out how he would die and what others would do with his clothes as he hung on his cross.

God's predictions, made centuries before Jesus came along, gave great hope to people that God's Christ *would* come. And to us, as people who are alive after Jesus lived and died, they can actually give great confidence that in Jesus, to whom all God's predictions happened, God's Christ *has* come.

Yes, but...

surely Jesus didn't really rise?

One of Jesus' earliest followers, Paul, wrote that: **"If Christ has not been raised ... faith is useless."** *

The resurrection of Jesus back to life is the place where the whole of Christianity stands or falls. And the resurrection of Jesus is the place where lots of people say: "That's just ridiculous. The rest of the story, OK—but not a dead man coming back to life!"

Let's be clear. No one can prove beyond any doubt that Jesus rose from the dead. But that's because no one can prove anything beyond any doubt. I can't prove my wife loves me—but, based on the evidence, I believe that she does. You can't prove that you're not a kitten who's dreaming it's a human—but, based on the evidence, you believe that you're not (hopefully!)

So in thinking about whether Jesus rose or not, it's about what you think is the *most likely* explanation for what happened that day in history.

And people have come up with some pretty good explanations. Below are the best I've found. For each, I've laid out the explanation as well as I can, and then mentioned the questions that they don't really answer.

1. There was no empty tomb: the women went to the wrong one

The women were tired and upset when they saw where Jesus was laid. When they visited the body a couple of days later, they went

* 1 Corinthians 15 v 17 *(Contemporary English Version translation)*

to the wrong tomb. The body wasn't there, they put two and two together and made 648, and told everyone he'd been raised.

Unanswered questions:

- They weren't expecting him to rise. If you went to the wrong tomb, wouldn't you just find the right one, not announce a resurrection?!
- When Jesus' followers announced a month or so later that Jesus had risen, why didn't the authorities simply go to the tomb they'd put soldiers outside, get the body, and disprove the resurrection?

2. The tomb was empty because Jesus wasn't really dead

Jesus didn't die on the cross—he just fainted, and then came to in the cool tomb. He then spent time with his friends and ate and walked with them, and then went away and lived somewhere else. His friends assumed he'd gone to heaven, and started talking about the resurrection.

Unanswered questions:

- The Romans were good at crucifying people. Did they really think Jesus was dead when he wasn't?
- One of the soldiers near the cross stuck a spear into his side. Could a man who'd been stabbed in the heart survive without medical help for three days and then walk out?
- Could a man who'd been nailed to a cross go for a long walk with friends two days later?
- Why didn't the guards at the tomb notice Jesus limping out?

3. The tomb was empty because the body was taken by the authorities

The leaders knew Jesus had predicted his resurrection. So they moved the body to make sure there could be no scam by his followers. That left an empty tomb; and the disciples took advantage of this, or misunderstood this, and went around saying Jesus had risen.

Unanswered questions:

- If the authorities had the body, why didn't they produce it when people started believing Jesus had risen? That would have stopped the rumors of resurrection!

4. The tomb was empty because the body was taken by grave-robbers

Bodies weren't valuable, but grave-clothes were. So some grave-robbers stole the body. The tomb was left empty for the women to find, and a legend was born.

Unanswered questions:

- Why, when the empty tomb was discovered, were the valuable grave-clothes still there? Why hadn't the grave-robbers taken the only thing in the tomb that was of value?

5. The tomb was empty because the body was taken by the disciples

Jesus' followers had much to gain from a "resurrection". So they stole the body, announced the resurrection and said Jesus had appeared to them several times, and that he'd now gone away again, back to heaven. And the resurrection lie enabled them to set up a new religion—Christianity.

Unanswered questions:

- Could the disciples, who were terrified and had run away, really have managed to pull off stealing a body from under the noses of some Roman guards?
- If the disciples had made up the Gospels of Jesus in the Bible, why do they come across in them as scared, disloyal and weak? Wouldn't you make up something more impressive about yourself?

- If the disciples made this up, they knew for a fact Jesus hadn't risen. Yet almost all of them ended up being killed for saying he'd come back to life and was God. Wouldn't at least one of them have admitted it was all made up to avoid being crucified, stoned or beheaded?

6. The disciples didn't really see Jesus: it was a hallucination

The "appearances" of Jesus were simple hallucinations. After all, the disciples were emotional, tired and grieving—and they saw what they wanted to see.

Unanswered questions:

- Medically, people simply don't hallucinate the same thing at the same time. Did dozens (and on one occasion hundreds) of adults really have an identical hallucination at exactly the same time?
- Why was the tomb empty? If this was a hallucination, the body would still have been in the tomb.

7. The tomb was empty because Jesus had risen back to life

This is what Jesus' friends claimed had happened, even when they faced gruesome deaths for saying it. It explains the empty tomb; and it explains the appearances of Jesus after his death.

Unanswered questions:

- Do people really rise from the dead? It's not exactly a normal event! (To which my answer, for what it's worth, is that if you were God, you could raise someone from the dead without difficulty. And if you wanted to prove you were God, you'd need to do something amazing and abnormal—like promising to die and rise again, and then actually doing that.)

About the author

Carl Laferton (@CarlLaferton) worked as a
sports journalist and teacher before he joined
The Good Book Company as Senior Editor.
He's married to Lizzie and they have one
son, Benjamin. His greatest claim to fame is
that he's been banned from the press box at
Twickenham rugby stadium in London, UK.

thegoodbook
COMPANY

Opening up the Bible

At The Good Book Company, we are dedicated to helping people discover Christ, and to helping Christians and local churches grow. We believe that God's growth process always starts with hearing clearly what he has said to us through his timeless word—the Bible.

Ever since we opened our doors in 1991, we have been striving to produce resources that honor God in the way the Bible is used. We have grown to become an international provider of user-friendly resources to the Christian community, with believers of all backgrounds and denominations using our Bible studies, books, resources, DVD-based courses and training events.

We want to explain Christianity to those who are interested, and to equip ordinary Christians to live for Christ day by day, and churches to grow in their knowledge of God and their love for one another.

Call us for a discussion of your needs or visit one of our local websites for more information on the resources and services we provide.

US & Canada: www.thegoodbook.com
UK & Europe: www.thegoodbook.co.uk
Australia: www.thegoodbook.com.au
New Zealand: www.thegoodbook.co.nz

US & Canada: 866 244 2165
UK & Europe: 0333 123 0880
Australia: (02) 6100 4211
New Zealand (+64) 3 343 1990

www.christianityexplored.org

Our partner site is a great place for anyone exploring the Christian faith, with a clear explanation of the good news, powerful testimonies and answers to difficult questions.

One life. What's it all about?